I Can Write Cursive

Brighter Child®
An imprint of Carson-Dellosa Publishing LLC
P.O. Box 35665
Greensboro, NC 27425 USA

10 11 12 13 14 15 HPS 15 14 13 12 11 10

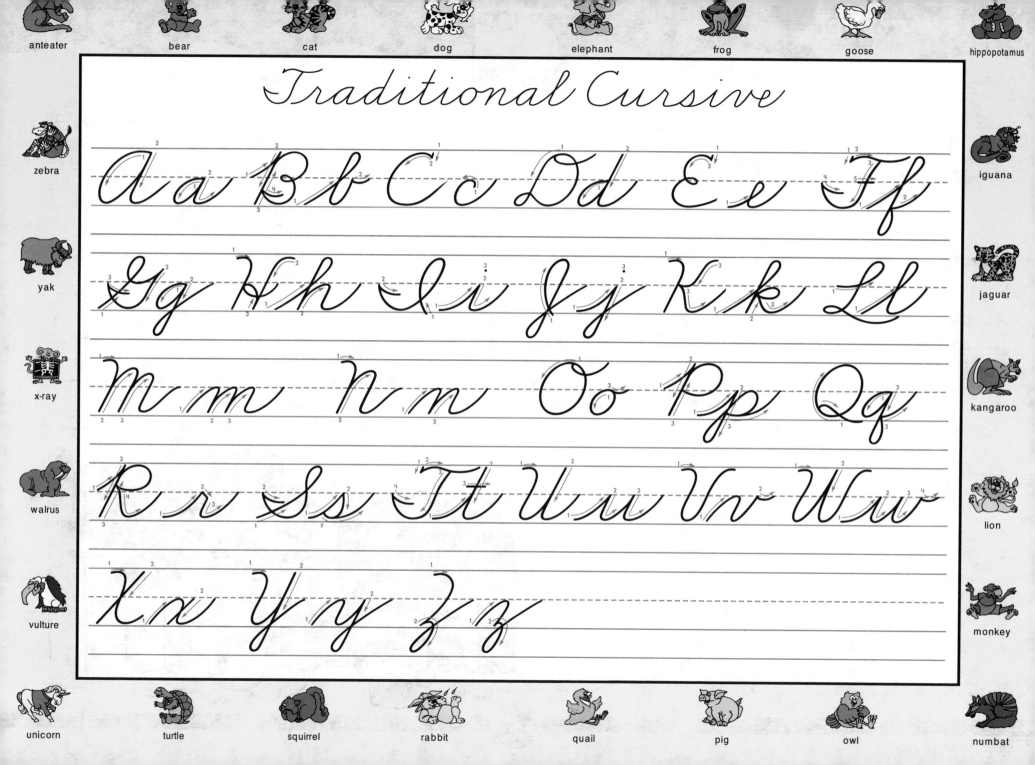

Traditional Cursive

Aa Bb Cc Dd Ee Ff
Gg Hh Ii Jj Kk Ll
Mm Nn Oo Pp Qq
Rr Ss Tt Uu Vv Ww
Xx Yy Zz

anteater bear cat dog elephant frog goose hippopotamus

zebra iguana

yak jaguar

x-ray kangaroo

walrus lion

vulture monkey

unicorn turtle squirrel rabbit quail pig owl numbat

Let's Warm Up!

Practice by tracing the lines.

Name _____

Let's Warm Up!

Practice by tracing the lines.

Name _____

Let's Warm Up!

Practice by tracing the lines.

Let's Warm Up!

Practice by tracing the lines.

Name _____

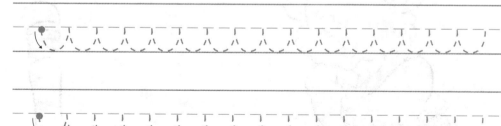

Practice by tracing the lines.

Name _____

Practice by tracing the lines.

Name _____

Aa

Practice by tracing the letter.
Then write the letter.

Name _____

a a a a a

a a a a a

Aa

Practice by tracing the words.
Then write the words.

an

and

animals

April

Write the phrase.

Name _____

Arctic animals

act amusingly

Aa

Write the sentence.

Name _____

Arctic animals act amusingly.

Bb

Practice by tracing the letter.
Then write the letter.

Bb

Practice by tracing the words.
Then write the words.

big

boy

babble

baboon

Write the phrase.

Name _____

Big baboons

break balloons

Write the sentence.

Name _____

Big baboons break balloons.

Practice by tracing the letter.
Then write the letter.

Name _____

C C C C C

c c c c c

Cc

Practice by tracing the words.
Then write the words.

can

candy

cool

count

Cc

Name _____

Cool crocodiles

count coconuts

Write the sentence.

Name _____

Cool crocodiles count coconuts.

Dd

Practice by tracing the letter.
Then write the letter.

Name _____

Dd

Practice by tracing the words.
Then write the words.

Name _____

do

dog

dandelions

donuts

DELIVERY

Write the phrase.

Dogs deliver

dandelions and donuts

Write the sentence.

Name _____

Dogs deliver dandelions and donuts.

Practice by tracing the letter.
Then write the letter.

Name _____

Ee

Practice by tracing the words.
Then write the words.

Name _____

each

eat

eels

eighty

Write the phrase.

Name _____

Electric eels

eat excitedly

Write the sentence.

Name _____

Electric eels eat excitedly.

Practice by tracing the letter.
Then write the letter.

Name _____

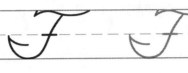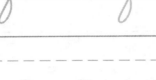

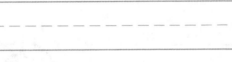

Practice by tracing the words.
Then write the words.

Name _____

far

fat

fluff

Flamingos fluff

fancy feathers

Write the sentence.

Name _____

Flamingos fluff fancy feathers.

Practice writing on your own.

Name _____

Practice Page

Practice writing on your own.

Name _____

Practice writing on your own.

Name _____

Practice writing on your own.

Name _____

Gg

Practice by tracing the letter.
Then write the letter.

Name _____

Gg

Practice by tracing the words.
Then write the words.

gag

gift

good

giggle

Gg

Write the phrase.

Giggling gophers

gag gifts

Gg

Write the sentence.

Giggling gophers give gag gifts.

Practice by tracing the letter.
Then write the letter.

Name _____

$\mathcal{H}$ $\mathcal{H}$ $\mathcal{H}$ $\mathcal{H}$ $\mathcal{H}$

h h h h h

Hh

Practice by tracing the words.
Then write the words.

his

happy

he

hello

Write the phrase.

Name _____

Happy hippos

hang hammocks

Write the sentence.

Name _____

Happy hippos hang in their hammocks.

Practice by tracing the letter.
Then write the letter.

Name _____

Practice by tracing the words.
Then write the words.

Name _____

if

in

idea

itch

Name _____

Insects itch

in infield

Write the sentence.

Name _____

Insects itch in the infield.

Jj

Practice by tracing the letter.
Then write the letter.

Name _____

$\mathcal{J}$ $\mathcal{J}$ $\mathcal{J}$ $\mathcal{J}$ $\mathcal{J}$

j j j j j

Practice by tracing the words.
Then write the words.

Name _____

jam

job

jazz

junk

Write the phrase.

Name _____

Juggling jaguars

to jazz

Write the sentence.

Name _____

Juggling jaguars

jam to jazz.

Kk

Practice by tracing the letter.
Then write the letter.

Name _____

K K K K K

k k k k k

Kk

Practice by tracing the words.
Then write the words.

kid

key

Kick

keep

Kk

Write the phrase.

Kooky kangaroos

kick karate

Write the sentence.

Name _____

Kooky kangaroos kick in karate.

Practice by tracing the letter.
Then write the letter.

Name _____

L L L L L

l l l l l

Practice by tracing the words.
Then write the words.

Name _____

low

land

lamb

little

Write the phrase.

Name _____

Little lambs

lemon lollipops

Write the sentence.

Name _____

Little lambs lick lemon lollipops.

Practice writing on your own.

Name _____

Practice writing on your own.

Name _____

Practice writing on your own.

Name _____

Practice writing on your own.

Name _____

Mm

Practice by tracing the letter.
Then write the letter.

m m m m m

m m m m m

Mm

Practice by tracing the words.
Then write the words.

mad

milk

monkeys

merry

Mm

Write the phrase.

Name _____

Merry monkeys

make marmalade

Mm

Merry monkeys make marmalade.

Nn

Practice by tracing the letter.
Then write the letter.

n n n n n

m m m m m

Nn

Practice by tracing the words.
Then write the words.

nap

name

near

night

Write the phrase.

Name _____

naughty gnats

never nap

Write the sentence.

Name _____

Naughty gnats never nap at night.

Practice by tracing the letter.
Then write the letter.

Name _____

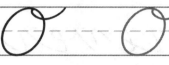

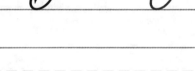

Practice by tracing the words.
Then write the words.

Name _____

out

often

once

order

Write the phrase.

Name _____

Ostriches often

onion omelettes

Oo

Name _____

Ostriches often order onion omelettes.

MENU

egg omelette

77

Pp

Practice by tracing the letter.
Then write the letter.

Name _____

P P P P P P

p p p p p

Pp

Practice by tracing the words.
Then write the words.

Name _____

pan

pet

pick

paper

Write the phrase.

Name _____

Pandas paint

pictures paper

Pp

Name _____

Pandas paint pictures on paper.

Qq

Practice by tracing the letter.
Then write the letter.

Q Q Q Q Q

q q q q q

Qq

Practice by tracing the words.
Then write the words.

Name _____

quit

quick

quart

quiet

Qq

Name _____

Quick quails

unique quarter

Write the sentence.

Name _____

Quick quails quarrel over a unique quarter.

Rr

Practice by tracing the letter.
Then write the letter.

Name _____

 R R R R

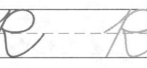 N N N N

Practice by tracing the words.
Then write the words.

Name _____

rat

run

rear

road

Write the phrase.

Name _____

Raccoons run

red cars

Rr

Name _____

Raccoons run races
in red cars.

Practice writing on your own.

Name _____

Practice writing on your own.

Name _____

Practice writing on your own.

Name _____

Practice writing on your own.

Name _____

Ss

Practice by tracing the letter.
Then write the letter.

Name _____

Ss

Practice by tracing the words.
Then write the words.

Name _____

see

sing

stand

stow

Ss

Write the phrase.

Name _____

Standing storks

sing swans

Write the sentence.

Name _____

Standing storks

sing with swans.

Practice by tracing the letter.
Then write the letter.

Name _____

Practice by tracing the words.
Then write the words.

Name _____

the

tip

told

twist

Write the phrase.

Name _____

Two tigers

tickle toes

Write the sentence.

Name _____

Two tigers tickle the other's toes.

Uu

Practice by tracing the letter.
Then write the letter.

Name _____

Uu

Practice by tracing the words.
Then write the words.

use

under

until

unhappy

Write the phrase.

Name _____

Unicorns use

umbrellas under

Uu

Name _____

Unicorns use umbrellas under thunder.

Vv

Practice by tracing the letter.
Then write the letter.

Name _____

$\mathcal{V}$ $\mathcal{V}$ $\mathcal{V}$ $\mathcal{V}$ $\mathcal{V}$

$\mathcal{v}$ $\mathcal{v}$ $\mathcal{v}$ $\mathcal{v}$ $\mathcal{v}$

Practice by tracing the words.
Then write the words.

Name _____

very

vote

vine

vest

Vv

Name _____

Vultures vacuum

velvet vests

Write the sentence.

Name _____

Vultures vacuum in velvet vests.

Ww

Practice by tracing the letter.
Then write the letter.

Name _____

$\mathcal{W}$ $\mathcal{W}$ $\mathcal{W}$ $\mathcal{W}$ $\mathcal{W}$

w w w w w

Ww

Practice by tracing the words.
Then write the words.

wet

west

wall

winter

Ww

Name _____

Wet walruses

to win

Ww

Write the sentence.

Wet walruses bowl
to win.

Xx

Practice by tracing the letter.
Then write the letter.

Name _____

$\mathscr{X}$ $\mathscr{X}$ $\mathscr{X}$ $\mathscr{X}$ $\mathscr{X}$

$\mathscr{x}$ $\mathscr{x}$ $\mathscr{x}$ $\mathscr{x}$ $\mathscr{x}$

Practice by tracing the words.
Then write the words.

Name _____

x-ray

box

extra

xylophone

X-RAY
MACHINE

Write the phrase.

Name _____

x-ray boxes

with foxes

Xx

Name _____

Xandra x-rays

boxes with foxes.

X-RAY
MACHINE

Yy

Practice by tracing the letter.
Then write the letter.

Name _____

Y Y Y Y Y

y y y y y

Yy

Practice by tracing the words.
Then write the words.

you

yard

year

yellow

Write the phrase.

Name _____

Yaks yell

Yodel loudly

Write the sentence.

Name _____

Yaks yell and yodel loudly.

Practice by tracing the letter.
Then write the letter.

Name _____

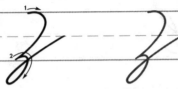 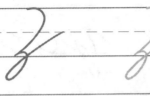 

Zz

Practice by tracing the words.
Then write the words.

zero

zoom

zone

zipper

Zz

Write the phrase.

Name _____

zigzagging zebras

zip zoom

Zz

Write the sentence.

Name _____

Zigzagging zebras zip and zoom.

Practice writing on your own.

Name _____

Practice writing on your own.

Name _____

Practice writing on your own.

Name _____